A Quarter Past Normal

A Quarter Past Normal

The Art of Redemption

By Linda Price

ISBN 978-1-7923-8241-3

Front cover image, back cover image, and book design by the author.

Printed in the United States of America

www.rock-paper-fortress.com

Dedicated to
Tom Hawkins,
my teacher, my mentor,
my cheerleader,
my friend

Introduction

A Quarter Past Normal is a visual and written testimony of the power of redemption—the restoration of dignity and divine purpose that God intended for each one of us to embrace, in spite of deep wounds from our pasts, personal human failings, dishonored existences, and bondage to fear and shame.

The truth is, I lived most of my life not knowing that I needed rescuing, even though many of my childhood ponderings included plans to end my life—or at least to somehow disappear from it. It never occurred to me that this kind of thinking was abnormal. As an adult, I was unaware that I had been chronically abused as a child, had lived my life secretly paralyzed by shame, and had somehow learned to protect my original identity within unseen, impenetrable walls inside my mind. I trusted no one, except for God. I believed that this, too, was normal. My life looked normal on the outside, which is what kept me in denial for years.

As a thriving artist, writer, teacher, wife, and mother, I was unaware of the depth of woundedness hidden in my soul. I successfully bounced through life as a happy camper for decades, outwardly productive and upbeat, while inwardly desperate and lost. This scenario worked reasonably well for the most part, until an accumulation of the violations to my body, soul, and spirit as a child eventually surfaced and could no longer be ignored. Suddenly, I didn't feel normal anymore. And that, from a human perspective, is when my redemption began—at "a quarter past normal."

Two central truths are emphasized in the book, *A Quarter Past Normal*. The first is that God's love is powerful enough and persistent enough—with or without our personal invitation—to expose the deception in our hearts and minds that has left us living in brokenness. The second truth is that by courageously facing our deepest fears, anger, and shame head-on, we dismantle the confusion, pain, and denial that have controlled our self-defeating thoughts and behavior for decades. Wounded souls don't usually heal on their own, although with God, anything is possible. Deeply wounded people who come to realize that "something is wrong, and I just want to fix it" need to be heard, seen, understood, and liberated from their woundedness through compassionate, objective, outside intervention. The longer our deepest pain is shoved away—deliberately or unconsciously—the more it controls our thoughts and behavior and robs us of joy. I understand this scenario intimately; it is the story of my life, and that of the generations preceding me.

I have the deepest admiration for specialists in the mental health care field and inner healing ministries who have followed their calling to bring emotionally, mentally, and spiritually despondent fighters back to life. These are the people who literally saved my life. Without them, the artwork in this book would never have been created, and the book itself would never have been written.

A Quarter Past Normal is a collection of original art and poetry created before, during, and after my journey of healing from an unremembered childhood. Some of this work has been featured in newspaper articles, public and private art shows, written publications about inner healing, doctors' offices, and therapists' conferences. Although the therapeutic art included in this book has been well-received by even the general public, it is featured here mainly to validate and encourage abuse survivors to use their creativity as an outlet for feeling and healing. Unrestrained art and writing have a way of connecting an individual with their true essence and increasing their capacity to live life and give life, even as they are engaged in the ongoing process of healing.

Due to this emphasis, the target audience of *A Quarter Past Normal* includes the broad community of people involved in inner healing—counselors, therapists and other mental health professionals, pastors, support people, and, most of all, survivors of abuse. And yet, this book may also speak to seemingly "normal" individuals who might suddenly recognize pieces of their own lives on these pages and consider that they, too, have a story that needs to be heard.

One key feature of *A Quarter Past Normal* is "the story behind" each piece of art and poetry, included on the page following or opposite the featured artwork or poem. It is within these brief summaries that my personal story of brokenness, truth encounters, and healing has been interwoven. I haven't included the gory details from my past. But I have revealed enough of my story for the reader to grasp the depth of dysfunction within my family of origin that allowed ongoing, severe abuse to occur inside and outside our home. More importantly, I have included enough of my story to convey the invaluable impact of spiritual and human intervention in restoring wholeness to deeply wounded souls.

The primary goal of healing from childhood and adult woundedness isn't just to stop living out of fear or to learn to accept yourself or to get your life back, although these reasons are—in and of themselves—worth the time and effort. The primary goal of inner healing goes even further than proactively opposing the attacks of the Enemy, who seeks to steal, kill, and destroy. From my personal perspective, the primary goal of inner healing is to reclaim the purposeful life God designed for you so that *you*—no matter what your age or gender, strengths or weaknesses, accomplishments or failures, profession or calling, or any other attribute—can be a life-giver to others. We are each made in God's image and, as His sons and daughters, are designed to change lives.

"The thief comes only to steal, kill, and destroy;
I came that they may have life,
and have it abundantly."

John 10:10

Table of Contents – Artwork and Poetry

*"Speak up for those who cannot speak
for themselves, for the rights of
all who are destitute."*

Proverbs 31:8

A Quarter Past Normal

It's a quarter past normal,
  and you have rudely awakened me
    to things I don't want to know.
I thought I was graced
  with a life simpler than yours—
    shorter in memory,
      though deeper in feelings.
Here, there, a little bit of
  everywhere
      and nowhere
          all at once.
And though I told you
  my childhood was lost,
I didn't realize you
  would take it as a question
    that had to be answered.
And the answers keep coming,
  but most of them don't seem to fit me.
    Only little bits and pieces
remind me of things I have never known
  but often pondered
    somewhere deep inside.

"Blue Girl"

The Story Behind *A Quarter Past Normal* – After listening to my summation of the dynamics in my family of origin, my first therapist commented that it wasn't normal to mentally block out the memory of entire portions of your past. She also said it wasn't normal to spend your entire life wishing you were dead. And so, my journey began.

The title poem, *A Quarter Past Normal*, was written several months after I had begun meeting with this therapist. I learned that my personal recollection of childhood was a conglomeration of "bits and pieces" of people, places, and events from my past, trapped in separate parts of my mind. These parts—created by my young, despairing, unconscious mind—allowed me to function outwardly as a creative, intelligent, well-adjusted child. In the process of therapy, God used my artwork and poetry to help me unite the fragmented thoughts and images floating in my mind into a cohesive understanding of my childhood experience.

The Story Behind *Blue Girl* – This painting was created several years after I began therapy, soon before I was healed. My children had encouraged me to enter a local art competition, so I decided to create a piece of contemporary art that also represented my journey of healing. The title and the ambiance of *Blue Girl* was inspired by Gainsborough's *The Blue Boy*. The cool, subdued tones in *Blue Girl* contrast with the warm, reflected light on the girl's face—representing how God's truth illuminates the darkness of our human understanding. The floating shapes in the background are distorted, topsy-turvy hearts, symbolizing the girl's conflicted emotions. Following the art show, an elementary school counselor bought this painting for her home.

The Story Behind *Someone Stands in the Way* – This watercolor painting was created two years after I started therapy. I had become aware of several distinct parts of my mind that had helped me function in the real world as a "normal" human being. Each of these parts held information about my past.

One young inside part seemed especially unreachable, as represented by the physical and emotional distance shown between the two girls in this painting. The question posed in the first line of the poem asks who, exactly, is the "someone" who stands in the way. Is the young woman standing in the way of acknowledging her deeply buried shame by pushing away the child who carries it? Or is the child standing in the way of connecting with the woman because of her fear, anger, or shame? They both need healing, but who needs to let go? After displaying this painting at a private art show for survivors, a family physician bought it for his office so his patients would feel free to talk about their *real* problems.

Someone stands in the way
     of the memories, the feelings, the healing.
Her strength is her weakness;
     her resolve will tear her down.
Because even though her boldness and sureness and strongmindedness
     carried her through life's hurts long ago,
          that was long ago, and this is now.
And the hurt will keep hurting
               until she lets go.

"Someone Stands in the Way"

The psychiatrist overseeing the Christian therapy practice where I began my counseling focused on two main issues from my past. First, that I was sexually assaulted as a teenager by an Air Force colonel who was a neighbor and a close family friend. (I had never before disclosed this secret). Second, that I had mentally blocked out most of the memories from the first 14 years of my life.

In looking back, I now know that my psychiatrist didn't grasp the full significance of large blocks of time erased from one's past. Underestimating the significance of what I *did* remember, he naïvely suggested that I could resolve my issues during two weeks of intensive inpatient therapy. This was long before the therapeutic community as a whole accepted the reality and pervasiveness of dissociative disorders. Although I winced at the thought of being labeled a "psych patient" for the rest of my life, I also knew that God had intentionally provided this path of healing.

The art on these two pages was created as part of my inpatient therapy work. Since I lacked the memories and emotions necessary for writing in the journal I'd been given, I began producing art as a means of getting in touch with the blank spots from my childhood. Creating art in the presence of strangers was stressful because of my insecurities as an artist. My giftedness had never been acknowledged by my parents, so I doubted that I had any talent at all. And yet, in therapy, my art flowed because my soul needed to speak.

The pastel drawings on this page and the collage on the opposite page depict how I felt when I tried to get in touch with the abuse I experienced as a child. The drawing on the opposite page of the boy and girl falling through a maze of lines and cubes represents my initial awareness of having parts in my mind that held different pieces of knowledge from my past. The painting of the girl looking at the empty swing epitomizes the years I spent not being fully present in my own life, because I was too busy trying to escape it.

The Story Behind *Broken Little Girl* – If you look closely, it's possible to know part of a person's story by looking into their eyes. This is apparent in the eyes of the *Broken Little Girl*, validated by the words of the poem. I originally drew this young child whole and unbroken, with a simple neutral background. The drawing was a term art project for a photographic rendering course in college. The original portrait—drawn with conté sticks—was the only piece of art I kept from my college days.

Fifteen years later, after beginning therapy, I noticed that my artwork was warping under the glass of its frame. I carefully took apart the frame and began to remove the drawing from its cardboard backing. To my horror, the portrait ripped at the little girl's left elbow. I gasped in disbelief. Then I looked up at God and said, "Please fix this." I had always believed that God was directly responsible for my best art—felt as if His hands were literally reaching through mine as I worked. And now I needed Him to help me redeem my most prized drawing.

Immediately, I began to consider how I might transform this damaged portrait into a powerful representation of my shattered childhood. I carefully ripped the drawing of the little girl in two more places and glued all the pieces onto a heavy piece of watercolor paper. Next, I created the background with watercolors and conté, leaving a large empty space for a poem I was planning in my head. I painted the obscure forest in the background to symbolize the unknown aspects of my childhood. Torn-paper hearts and flowers were added in the foreground to epitomize the façade my family presented to the outside world.

The poem *Broken Little Girl* was written one afternoon while I was completing this restored work of art. As I hand-lettered the poem onto the painting, I remembered what it felt like as a child to *not* see, *not* hear, and *not* feel sadness and shame. To the outside world, I had appeared to be an average, well-adjusted child because my mind and emotions were too disconnected for the truth to register on my face.

One important lesson I learned in my adulthood was that, although God didn't plan for me to suffer at the hands of the Enemy, He permitted it as part of His overriding purposes for my life. He allowed me to feel damaged, rejected, and worthless so I would be forced to depend upon Him alone for my sense of honor and legitimacy. And He gave me the ability to look far beyond my losses so I could tell the story that needed to be told.

More prints of *Broken Little Girl* have been sold than any other piece of my artwork, probably because its story is so universal. Whether or not you look like this little girl, whether you're a man or a woman, a child or an adult, whether you are seeking the truth or living in denial of it, if you have suffered deeply at the hands of people who should have valued you, this child's story might be yours, as well.

A little girl lived long ago
In worlds unknown to me;
She wandered through
        a daydream land
That no one else could see.

She learned to look
        with vacant eyes,
She heard with
        deafened ears;
And somehow she
        remained a child
Through all the
        silent years.

The little girl of long ago
Is someone you can't see;
But underneath her brokenness
I'm sure that you'll find me.

"Broken Little Girl"

Waiting for Dad

I know my dad will come some day
        to take me in his arms,
Though now he is too far away
        to keep me from life's harm.
I know that somewhere deep inside
        he's very close to me,
And if I wait here long enough,
        he'll come eventually.

I'm sure my dad must know that I
        am waiting here for him,
And though I don't know why he's gone
        I'll wait through thick and thin.
For even if he cannot see
        the sadness in my eyes,
I know he feels it in his heart
        because he's very wise.

So though the sun shall rise and set
        and clouds shall come and go,
And though it seems forever til
        he comes, this much I know:
That even if I'm old and gray
        or still quite young and free,
My father will come home someday
        in time to rescue *me*.

Waiting for Dad

I know my dad will come some day
to take me in his arms,
Though now he is too far away
to keep me from life's harm.
I know that somewhere deep inside
he's very close to me;
And if I wait here long enough,
he'll come eventually.

I'm sure my dad must know that I
am waiting here for him;
And though I don't know why he's gone,
I'll wait through thick and thin.
For even if he cannot see
the sadness in my eyes,
I know he feels it in his heart
because he's very wise.

So though the sun shall rise and set
and clouds shall come and go,
And though it seems forever til
he comes, this much I know:
That even if I'm old and gray
or still quite young and free,
My father will come home someday
in time to rescue me.

"Waiting for Dad"

The Story Behind *Waiting for Dad* – Long before I decided to enter therapy, God gave me a yearning for the truth. Even as a child, I was always trying to figure out what was really going on around me. I grew up feeling "different" and separate from my family. One day God allowed the pressures in my adult life to force me to face some secrets from my past. My body suddenly began showing signs of severe, early childhood abuse, yet I had no memories to account for these symptoms. Eventually I had to face the fact that something was terribly wrong.

That's when I contacted a therapist to help me address the one violent memory I could recall—a sexual assault as a teenager. My decision to talk about my past with an outsider met with such vehement opposition from my parents and siblings that I was "severed" (my father's term) from their lives

for the next 20 years. But because I knew that my dad loved me, I hoped his heart would soften and he would tell me he understood my need to get help. Yet he and my family ceased communication with me and kept their distance for the next two decades.

Waiting for Dad expresses a childish wish I knew would never come true—that my dad would save us all from our family's secret prison of deception and shame. But when I realized that my dad *couldn't* save us—when it finally became clear to me that *he* was a big part of the problem, I stopped waiting for him to show up. God took my father's place as my shield, my glory, and the lifter of my head (Psalm 3:3). After years of looking back at a never-ending childhood that had been neither beautiful nor innocent, God healed my wounded soul, restoring an integrated sense of identity to my existence.

11

The Story Behind *The Yellow Shovel* – At first glance, *The Yellow Shovel* appears to be a tender painting of a carefree little girl enjoying a day at the beach. The sun is high, the clouds are brilliant, and the child is playing contentedly, dressed in a stylish swimsuit, with her hair pulled back neatly into a ponytail. She is trying out her (barely visible) new yellow shovel, which is perfect and wonderful and hers alone.

Not long after completing this painting, I found myself looking at this little girl from a totally different viewpoint. Suddenly, her tiny, solitary presence—with her back to the viewer and surrounded only by land, air, and water—made her seem isolated and defenseless. This unexpected shift in my perspective made me realize how profoundly woundedness can affect a person's interpretation of the world around them. Unresolved, buried pain can diminish the ability to experience joy. It influences whether we spend our lives actively seeking to connect with others or secretly trying to hide from them. It affects how we see life and how we remember it.

Individuals who grow up in reasonably healthy homes and who have a connected sense of personal history may find it difficult to understand how anyone could mentally block out entire years or events from their past. And yet, survivors who have done so grow up assuming that it's normal *not* to have complete memories, because that's all they've ever known.

In my case, my unremembered past was broken up by mental "blips" of feelings and pictures that "pinged" off my mind— fragmented images such as playing board games with my siblings, dreading family vacations, feeling invisible and absent in our home, my grandmother's enduring love, my father's erratic restraint, my mother's terrorizing rage, my favorite elementary school teachers, and recurring nightmares of trying to get away. As represented by the little girl with the yellow shovel, I spent much of my childhood surrounded by life but not engaged in it, except for my unwavering connection to God.

This brings up the matter of God's intercession in the context of injustice in the world. Many survivors struggle with the thought that God abandoned them as children during their time of greatest need. They believe that God should have protected them from the abusive people and the injustices in their childhood. But even though God *is* in control of the universe and knows exactly what He's doing, governing human behavior *isn't* a part of His plan. Adam and Eve are proof of this. And because of their decision to listen to Satan and disregard God, sin— which became a part of every human being's existence—initiated the suffering, injustice, and death that is in our world. Nevertheless, even in our agony, when God says that He is with us, He is *with* us.

"For I am persuaded that neither death, nor life, nor angels, nor principalities, nor powers, nor things present, nor things to come, nor height, nor depth, nor any other creature shall be able to separate us from the love of God, which is in Christ Jesus our Lord."

Romans 8:38-39

"The Yellow Shovel"

Awakening

And if a storm
should suddenly knock you off your feet
and toss you to the uttermost parts
of the earth,
If the strength of its gales
should dismantle your foundation
and turn your world upside down
and leave you wandering…
…wondering where you had come from
and what you had endured
and what part of your original self
might still be intact,
If you should suddenly open your eyes
to the frightening unfamiliarity
of your surroundings
or the signs of intrusion
or the absence of all understanding
as if you had just begun to exist,
then you might understand
where I have been
and what divided our worlds
and why I must find my way through
the silent wall that lies between us.

"After the Storm"

The Story Behind *Awakening* – The poem *Awakening* was written towards the end of my therapy, when I was trying to describe for other people on their own journeys what it is like to suddenly "wake up" and realize that the life you thought was yours was only a partial, "acceptable version" of the life that you actually lived. It expresses what it can feel like to discover hidden aspects of your identity that don't make sense—and then, suddenly, they do. The upheaval of such a revelation can either drag you backwards, launch you forward, or stop you in your tracks. I am living proof that God is in the active process of setting prisoners free—no matter how dark or shameful or fragmented their pasts, no matter how much time it takes to put the pieces back together again.

The Story Behind *After the Storm* – This acrylic painting was created for a silent auction in Austin, Texas. I had contributed several paintings to this non-profit organization over the years, but this ended up being one of my favorites. The random items shown on the beach are typical of those found scattered along almost any coastal shore after a storm. But the debris shown here also symbolizes the fragments of images and thoughts found in the shattered minds of people who have survived tremendous pain and suffering from an early age. The quiet, watchful mourning dove—one of my favorites of God's creations—represents the years I spent watching my life drift by without realizing that I wasn't fully living it.

The Story Behind *Search Me* – The pencil drawing of the woman on the right, illustrating Psalm 139:23-24, was printed in a publication of the church I attended as a young adult. For a period of ten years, I was given the privilege and freedom of creating original drawings for my church's weekly bulletin covers. I chose whatever scripture inspired me and illustrated it however God led. However, as a result of growing up in an oppressive, shame-based home, I didn't recognize my skills as an artist, mostly because my work was marginalized by my parents, whose opinions I blindly trusted. Yet I knew that *other* people admired my work, which is why I continued to draw and paint. This bulletin cover is especially meaningful to me because it was drawn six years *before* I entered therapy. Even though I didn't know that something was "off" with my socially dynamic, devout Christian family, even when I didn't recognize that my mind was fragmented and my heart was devastated, I longed for God to show me who I was and define the path He had prepared for me.

Search me, O God, and know my heart;
try me, and know my anxieties;
and see if there is any wicked way in
me, and lead me in the way everlasting.

Psalm 139: 23, 24

Walls of Stone

There was a child who was so mild
That no one thought of her as wild.
And yet beneath her gentle face
Was chaos time could not erase.

And every day her pain would stay
Just out of reach, in no one's way.
And though she smiled, her soul was riled
Because it had been long defiled.

Yet, unreleased, her pain increased
Until her deepest longings ceased.
And in her mind she built the kind
Of fortress no one else could find.

Now all alone, in walls of stone,
A young girl guards her fragile throne.
And nobody can hurt her there.
And nobody can show they care.

So pain presumtuously plods on
With fear the queen and rage the pawn.
They fight to shield and yet to free
The little girl I once called *me*.

There was a child who was so mild
That no one thought of her as wild.
And yet beneath her gentle face
Was chaos time could not erase.

And every day her pain would stay
Just out of reach, in no one's way.
And though she smiled, her soul was riled
Because it had been long defiled.

Yet, unreleased, her pain increased
Until her deepest longings ceased.
And in her mind she built the kind
Of fortress no one else could find.

Now all alone, in walls of stone,
A young girl guards her fragile throne.
And nobody can hurt her there,
And nobody can show they care.

So pain presumptuously plods on
With fear the queen and rage the pawn.
They fight to shield and yet to free
The little girl I once called Me.

"Walls of Stone"

The Story Behind *Walls of Stone* – This painting is a visual representation of the dynamic of dissociation. Society often sees an intelligent, high-functioning individual on the outside, but is blind to the wounded parts of his or her mind locked inside. When survivors speak about "walls" inside their minds—they refer to the impenetrable partitions that keep various aspects of their divided mind separate from one another. These walls—an extreme version of everyday "mental blocks"—keep overwhelming memories psychologically unavailable to the out-front "presenting person", until the walls eventually start breaking down and the truth starts leaking out.

The words of this poem reflect the little girl's inner conflicts—the need to stay hidden within the walls of her fortress so she can't be hurt, and yet, her deep longing for someone to validate her presence and her torment. Pain from the child's past fuels the buried rage of the young woman on the outside, who can't understand what drives her anger and despair.

The Story Behind *Triple Portrait* – The foundation of this drawing is the Bible passage that inspired it—Matthew 10:26-28. God led me to this Scripture when I first sought to understand what

had caused me to block out memories of my youth. I embraced this promise in my search for answers: "…There is nothing covered that will not be revealed and hidden that will not be known." I petitioned God to bring to my conscious awareness, piece by piece, the things from my childhood that I needed to know in order to heal and to get my life back. My steadfast motto became, "Let go and let God."

This self-portrait was drawn using two photographs from my childhood, when my sense of dignity had already been ransacked and shame fueled my fantasy of being permanently invisible. The expression in all three girls' eyes reflects the unintentional distrust I felt towards everyone—even the people who were kind to me. My soul vacillated between wanting to be seen and known and needing to remain anonymous and safe.

Drawn below the portraits of the three girls are random, disconnected images from the young woman's mind: a flight of stairs leading to an unknown destination, a broken-down wooden door, a window revealing a darkened, vacant room, and half-empty cardboard boxes filled with debris and discarded memories. These images fade into the Bible verses to illustrate my deep yearning to know the truth, speak the truth, and be set free by the truth

"...for there is nothing covered that will not be revealed,
and hidden that will not be known.
What I tell you in the darkness, speak in the light;
and what you hear whispered in your ear,
proclaim upon the housetops.
And do not fear those who kill the body,
but are unable to kill the soul ..."
Matthew 10: 26-28

"Triple Portrait"

"My Fortress"

"I will say of the Lord,
He is my refuge and fortress: my God;
in Him will I trust."

     Psalm 91:2

<u>The Story Behind *My Fortress*</u> – The drawing on the opposite page was the first of several I attempted in a sketchbook purchased the summer before I turned 17. This was decades before I recognized my gift as an artist. The trust conveyed in this young boy's eyes reflects my own confidence in God's desire to safeguard the deepest, strongest parts of us—our spirit and soul—the parts that hold us together, that keep our hope alive and can't be destroyed by harsh circumstances or people. Often God's vigilant care is felt rather than seen, and other times it manifests visibly, as demonstrated in the story below.

In the summer of 2001, I drove my teenage daughter and all of her belongings from a southern coastal Texas city up to Dallas, where she was preparing to attend college. This move was no small task; I had to rent a U-Haul truck with a trailer attached to the back to transport my daughter's car. I shouldn't have attempted this venture on my own since I was still recovering from a knee surgery six weeks earlier. Yet, with no other options, my daughter and I packed up her things, traipsed up and down numerous flights of stairs with boxes and furniture, and loaded the U-Haul by ourselves. I had never driven a truck before—let alone hauled a trailer or a car—so I was a nervous wreck by the time we set out for Dallas.

As soon as we entered the highway, I was gripped with terror that our trailer would detach from the truck and cause a major freeway accident. I prayed silently for God's protection and peace, yet I couldn't shake my underlying fear of having foolishly taken on a job too big for me. Out of the blue, I spotted an 18-wheeler with an empty flatbed about a quarter of a mile in front of us. The unusual camouflage paint job on the semi's cab—something I'd never seen before—had caught my attention. I told myself that the trucker had hauled far heavier loads than I was carrying and certainly knew what he was doing. So I kept my eyes focused on the semi; I didn't look at anything else around me for miles—not the landscape, not the surrounding traffic—just the cab of the truck.

My fear began to dissipate gradually. After an hour of driving, I suddenly noticed that the semi was no longer in front of me. I looked in my rearview mirror; it wasn't behind me, either. At some point during those sixty minutes of tense highway driving, two things had happened. First, my extreme fear of impending disaster had dissolved completely, and second, the semi had disappeared into thin air.

Immediately, I knew that the driver of the semi had been an angel. There is no other way to explain his sudden disappearance. Through the intervention of an angel, God revealed what it means to be a life-giving fortress—someone who is not influenced by threats of adversity, someone who empowers others to take on difficult situations and encounters, and someone who provides strength and shelter for the lost and weary. God is my fortress.

"Call to Me"

The Story Behind *Call to Me* – People's inside stories inspire the portraits I paint and draw. In each case, I try to capture an individual's most candid essence, mainly through the expression in their eyes. The fear conveyed by the young boy above mirrors how I used to feel in my youth, when unendurable shame forced my memories of childhood into nonexistence. This is when I learned how to become someone *other* than myself.

The young boy in *Call to Me* is part of the series of portraits I sketched as a teen. My mother's harsh judgment of anyone (including me) who didn't live up to her unattainable ideals launched me into devotedly drawing the faces of people from diverse backgrounds—individuals of different ages, ethnicities, physical features, etc.—inspired by photographs from magazines. It is both a miracle and a blessing that I managed to save this little sketchbook—tangible evidence of my uninhibited gift as a young artist, my passion for minimized people, and my boundless pursuit of authenticity.

"Call to me
and I will answer you and
show you great and mighty things
which you do not know.

Jeremiah 33:3

The Story Behind *The Dream* – The girl in *The Dream* <u>was</u> me. As a teenager, I felt lost and insignificant. My self-concept was loosely based upon unequal shares of God's love, my teachers' admiration, and my mother's criticism. Without an enduring foundation on which to build my hopes, envisioning a bright future felt like shooting in the dark. But like the girl in the poem, I eventually broke out of survival mode and began to dream.

I was in my late thirties when God revealed to me that my heart was deeply wounded. That's when I woke up and sought professional help to address the victimization, abuse, and shame that had secretly robbed me of life. I wish I had recognized my pain sooner. But even when I don't understand God's timing, I'm always confident that His ways are higher than my ways (Isaiah 55:9).

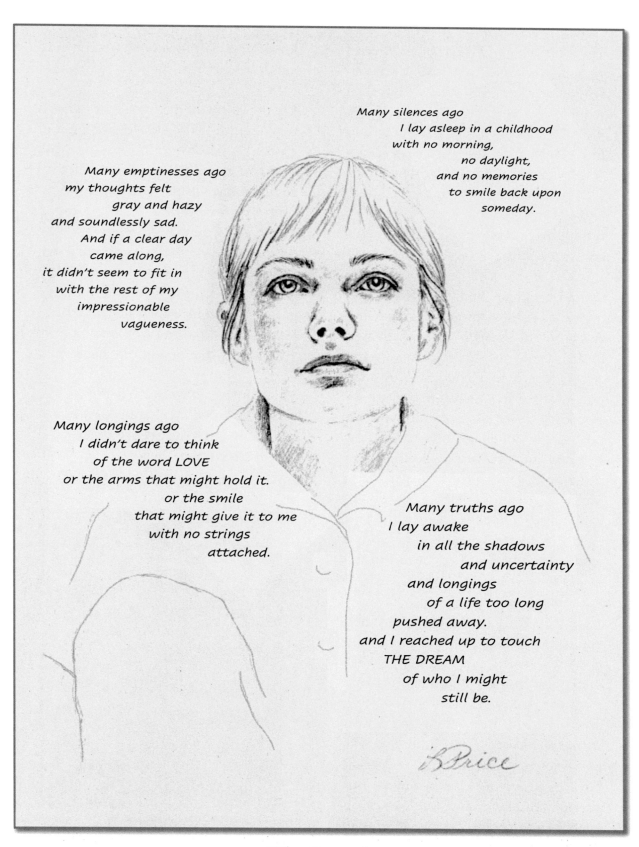

Many silences ago
    I lay asleep in a childhood
  with no morning,
       no daylight,
   and no memories
     to smile back upon
       someday.

Many emptinesses ago
my thoughts felt
   gray and hazy
and soundlessly sad.
  And if a clear day
  came along,
 it didn't seem to fit in
 with the rest of my
  impressionable
    vagueness.

Many longings ago
  I didn't dare to think
  of the word LOVE
or the arms that might hold it.
   or the smile
   that might give it to me
   with no strings
    attached.

Many truths ago
I lay awake
  in all the shadows
    and uncertainty
 and longings
   of a life too long
 pushed away.
and I reached up to touch
THE DREAM
  of who I might
    still be.

BPrice

"The Dream"

The Story Behind *Warrior* – Several years ago, I visited a private Christian school in San Antonio at which I would later become a teacher. While there, I met the young man pictured in the painting at the right—Aniekan, who was a history teacher at the school. Aniekan was humble, kind, and soft-spoken, yet I recognized an untapped aspect of this young man's enormous spirit.

On my way back home, I realized that my new Nigerian friend was unaware of the mighty warrior he was created to be. God prompted me to paint Aniekan as I envisioned his powerful potential for leadership and spiritual warfare. When Aniekan received his portrait, he got a big smile on his face. His roommates started shouting and cheering because they, too, perceived him as a warrior. This is one of my favorite portraits because it validated such an important aspect of this young man's identity that had been hidden from him previously.

The Story Behind *Abundance* – When you're raised in a shame-based family in which cruelty is continually swept under the rug, it's natural to become cynical and lose hope of ever feeling loved or safe. Part of me lived in a constant state of depression as I was growing up—quietly contemplating how to escape my circumstances. But part of me knew God was watching over me and protecting me—a simple,

life-giving truth firmly instilled by my Sunday School teachers.

My therapists helped me comprehend the magnitude of God's provision and grace. They helped me recognize that God had permitted my overwhelming circumstances as part of His prevailing purposes for my life. They equipped me to stop defining myself by how other people viewed me or treated me. I took ownership of my own fallibility and resisted the urge to continually judge my worst offenders. Finally, I learned how to forgive others with my will first, and then with my heart.

The painting *Abundance* represents the sense of freedom I gained when I recognized that my deep suffering and my extraordinary healing were both essential to my calling as a life-giver.

"Abundance"

"Warrior"

The Story Behind _Narnia_ – God's creation is a frequent theme in my paintings, although nature is far more challenging for me to paint than portraits of people. The nature motifs I use most often in my artwork are clouds, birds, flowers, and trees. My sons came home for a visit one weekend and saw this painting for the first time. It reminded them of the magical land of "Narnia" that Peter, Susan, Edmund, and Lucy discovered after entering the wardrobe in C.S. Lewis' popular allegory, _The Chronicles of Narnia_. This painting was dubbed _Narnia_ and has captured many hearts ever since.

The Story Behind _Wings of the Dawn_ – One image I remember as a child is staring at the clouds outside my bedroom window and talking to God—often. This may be when I began observing my own life from up above. _Wings of the Dawn_ was my first serious attempt at painting clouds. Even though I lacked confidence and expertise in portraying clouds with their intricate changes in light and form, the simplicity and innocence of this novice labor of love has made it one of my favorite paintings.

The Story Behind _Nigerian Sunrise_ – Ever since meeting my friend Aniekan, God has brought other Nigerian friends into my life whose genuineness and deep faith have been inspirational. I chose the title _Nigerian Sunrise_ after completing this painting, based upon its bold, vibrant colors, lyrical images of golden sunlight, and grounded energy of the solid black lines. The strength and balance of this painting remind me of the Hebrew name for God—"_El Shaddai_"—which means, "The All-Sufficient God."

"Narnia"

"Wings of the Dawn"

"Nigerian Sunrise"

"If I rise on the wings of the dawn,
if I settle on the far side of the sea,
even there your hand will guide me,
your right hand will hold me fast.
If I say, "Surely the darkness will hide me
and the light become night around me,"
even the darkness will not be dark to You;
the night will shine like the day,
for darkness is as light to You."

Psalm 139:9-12

29

Someone Else's Life

I am a vague reflection of
            all that is inside me –
a familiar face
            in a crowd
                of other faces,
    other thinkers,
            other dreamers.
    I try to be myself,
        though I'm never quite sure
            of who she is.
I hold on to the present
        by talking about the past
            as though it were
                someone else's life.
        Yet as I speak,
                my mind begins to drift,
            to wander back and forth
    across all the yesterdays
        which never belonged to me.
And suddenly I am gone,
        though not quite aware
            of my absence.
But you have seen the change,
        and you know
                that I am someone else
    who looks like me,
        but whose words tell
                a different story,
    and whose sadness
            is hers alone.

I am a vague reflection of
all that is inside me —
a familiar face
in a crowd
of other faces,
other thinkers,
other dreamers.
I try to be myself,
though I'm never quite sure
of who she is .
I hold on to the present
by talking about the past
as though it were
someone else's life .
Yet as I speak,
my mind begins to drift,
to wander back and forth
across all the yesterdays
which never belonged to me.
And suddenly I am gone,
though not quite aware
of my absence.
But you have seen the change,
and you know
that I am someone else
who looks like me,
but whose words tell
a different story,
and whose sadness
is hers alone.

J.Price

"Someone Else's Life"

The Story Behind *Someone Else's Life* –
Several weeks after I began therapy, I was diagnosed with DID—Dissociative Identity Disorder—a psychological anomaly in which a child responds to overwhelming, chronic abuse by mentally disconnecting from what is happening so she can survive in her everyday world. My medical diagnosis was based on several specific indicators, including the extensive gap in my memories of childhood, unexplainable bodily signs of severe past abuse, my obsession with dying, and the inaudible conversations that I mentioned taking place in my mind.

As a child, I learned how to "split off" awareness of the abuse I had endured by concealing it in different parts of my mind. These "parts"—of which I was completely unaware until buried emotions began to surface in adulthood—were aspects of my fragmented identity, each maintaining a specific age, gender, personality type, history of experiences, thoughts, behaviors, and internal functioning role (protector, negotiator, inner self-helper, etc.). In an undivided mind, these aspects of identity function as one integrated personality.

Someone Else's Life illustrates what it felt like during therapy when traumatic memories surfaced. At the beginning of a session, as long as the dialogue with my therapist felt familiar and safe, I stayed fully engaged and present in our conversation. But when the discussion shifted to past events which brought up feelings of deep despair, pain, or shame, I disconnected mentally and felt detached—like a stranger in my own body listening to someone else's story.

The Story Behind *Peace* – The painting below is one of my favorites because of its simplicity and elegance. It symbolizes the peace that was missing in my childhood and for most of my life. Before my journey of healing put me back on the path of life, I used to think that peace meant an absence of conflict—or that peace would result if cruel or deceptive people were exposed and punished. But I've since found that peace can come from putting to rest a harsh past and choosing a future without denial.

"Peace"

"On a Mission"

The Story Behind *On a Mission* – Some of the most unexpected happenings on the path out of pain and denial are the life-giving connections you make along the way. People who might not have synchronized with your uncertain, protected self effortlessly connect with your peaceful, healed presence. Upon completing my formal therapy sessions, God brought several women across my path whose personal honesty bolstered *my* transparency and the ability to trust.

As we began spending time together, I noticed many similarities between our journeys and purposes in life. Like me, each of these women had wrestled with deep pain and woundedness that had negatively affected them for years. Each had engaged in spiritual battles to overcome the Enemy's attempt to weaken their faith and sabotage their families. And each of these women had profound compassion for the struggling yet tenacious warriors that God had brought across their paths.

The painting *On a Mission* captures the essence of my friends' steadfastness and the message of Jeremiah 29:11, one of my most treasured Bible verses:

"For I know the plans I have for you,"
declares the Lord, "plans to prosper you
and not to harm you, plans to give you
hope and a future."

The Story Behind *Sara* – The watercolor painting *Sara* was one of a set of three illustrations I was commissioned to create for an author seeking to publish a children's book she had just completed. The realistic fictional book was targeted for middle school students and explored the life cycles and habits of ridley sea turtles; Sara was one of the main characters in the story. At that time, the book's author and I both worked in the English Department at Texas A&M University-Corpus Christi, a beautiful campus residing literally on an island. The author had just completed the text of her book and needed three sample illustrations to accompany the prototype she was sending to several publishers.

Two weeks after the prototypes had been mailed, the author excitedly came to me with a "rejection letter" from one of the publishers. "We're not publishing any chapter books at this time," the letter read, "but we'd really like to get in touch with your illustrator." I smiled and thanked my friend for sharing the letter with me. Not long after creating this illustration, I began my teaching career. One splendid year, my class of second graders included three Sara/Sarah's, one of whom looked exactly like the Sara in this illustration.

The Story Behind *Fun at the Beach* – This acrylic painting was created for a silent auction at a Dallas-area elementary school where I was a teacher. My inspiration was the frequent walks I'd taken along several South Texas beaches, where I often found interesting remnants of people's lives washed up on the shore. Yet the true significance of this painting occurred six years after its creation, when I lived in San Antonio and was scheduled to attend a teaching seminar in Corpus Christi.

Although I had previously lived in Corpus Christi for almost thirty years, when I finally moved away, I departed with unresolved cynicism due to a demoralizing marriage. I remember wishing that I could attend the seminar in a different city in which it was being offered, but I decided to face my fears and move ahead with the plan. Not surprisingly, God was a step ahead of me, preparing me for a big leap forward on my path of healing. As soon as I arrived in Corpus Christi, I suddenly realized that I had been blaming this city for the negative relationships I had experienced there years earlier. I decided to visit all of my old stomping grounds and bless the city and the land as beautiful displays of God's creation. It took me three days to complete my mission, and for the first time I felt at peace with the city where I had raised my children and begun my healing journey.

"Sara"

"Fun at the Beach"

"The Quarry"

The Story Behind *The Quarry* — This painting was created during one of my recent explorations of contemporary art. As with most of my abstract paintings, I launched this one without a plan, allowing the colors and shapes to lead the way. Paintings like this usually take me several days to complete and often emerge from many trial-and-error layers beneath the finished product. The result reminded me of one of my favorite shopping venues in Texas—*The Quarry*, in San Antonio. The tightly wedged, freeform shapes in this painting are representative of the intricate balance of weighty thoughts and emotions carried into therapy sessions. Sometimes, even the slightest shift in understanding can result in dramatic progress towards liberating your spirit and soul.

The Story Behind *On the Breakers* — In creating this painting, I incorporated a color palette similar to that used in *The Quarry*, but its purpose was totally different. Abstract expressionism, for me, provides a unique opportunity to relax my internal controls and let my emotions flow. It allows me the chance to take risks and create paintings with an unstructured, intuitive approach, while also achieving balance and harmony. The freedom to simply "feel" and "be" is liberatingly opposite of the rigid controls and rules that I experienced in my childhood home, which is why creating the painting, *On the Breakers*, felt so lifegiving to me.

"On the Breakers"

The Story Behind _New Beginnings_ and _Let There Be Life_. An unforeseen miracle happened a few years after I completed my journey of inner healing: My family of origin suddenly reentered my life. Sadly, it took my father's passing to bring us all back together again. Yet, regardless of our differences of opinion, in spite of the many missed birthdays, graduations, and weddings, notwithstanding the pain we had caused one another, God offered a precious gift to our family. He offered us the gift of restoration—the opportunity to humbly extend forgiveness and love to one another and to graciously redefine and rebuild our relationships. Although healing has been a gradual, diplomatic process, the essence of our redemption story is embodied in these two titles—_New Beginnings_ and _Let There Be Life_.

"New Beginnings"

"Let There Be Life"

37

The Story Behind *The Masterpiece* –
Many years ago I found a magazine ad featuring a forlorn, abandoned-looking child standing out in the field of a poverty-stricken country. Something about the young girl's despondent demeanor inspired me to paint her portrait—and rewrite her story. I knew that my portrait would be of a little girl, and I knew that she was going to be a budding artist; this was my only game plan. I wasn't sure of what, exactly, the little girl would look like when I was finished. But I knew that the expression on her face would be peaceful and assured. Without realizing it, I was rewriting the outcome of my own story through this compelling portrait.

Over a period of four years, the little girl on the canvas was gradually taking shape before my eyes. I spent hours perfecting the pensive expression in her eyes, the intricate interplay of light and shadows upon her face, and a sense of inner strength and humility in her posture. I strived to portray a modest child of mixed-race ethnicity so that a wider diversity of people could identify with her as an authentic and relatable person. When I finally finished my painting, I stood back and studied it closely. And suddenly, I realized that this little girl represented me as a child—not entirely convinced of my skills as a young artist, but unable to stop drawing and painting, simply because that's how God had designed me to be.

The title *The Masterpiece* was inspired by the manner in which the girl is standing back and contemplating a beautiful painting that she has just finished. She is both grateful and satisfied with her results. Yet the *real* masterpiece, of course, is the little girl, herself—a cherished and exquisite expression of God's perfect artistry.

Four years after completing this painting, I was hired as a long-term substitute teacher for a class of third graders in the Austin area. As soon as I met my class, I noticed that one of the students looked exactly like the young girl in my painting. When I showed her a photo of the artwork on my cell phone, she smiled shyly—just like the girl in *The Masterpiece*.

"The Masterpiece"

"Complete"

The Other Side of Denial

One day you wake up and realize
   that everything inside you
      is you.
All the fear, the innocence and pain,
   all the strength, the sadness and shame;
all the anger, the loveliness,
      the hurt and the longing;
everything that has touched your life,
   everything that shaped it,
everything that tore it down
      and all that has built it back up
         is you.

Suddenly you know
   that whatever needs to be said
      can be said by you.
Every feeling inside
      can be felt by you—
and you won't fall apart,
   and you won't disappear,
      and you won't be destroyed.

You realize
   that during all the years
      of wondering and praying,
   of pleading and searching
and running back and forth
   across the darkness and the light,
you were growing—
      growing up into the person
   God intended you to be.

One day you wake up
   and find that you are strong
      and brave,
   that you can hear the truth,
and you can face things that once
      stunned you into silence
   and scattered you across your world.
Then one by one,
   the walls come down.

And suddenly you find yourself
   sitting alone,
   embracing all you used to be.
And you know you are complete,
   and you wrap yourself in joy,
      and you cry.
And then you put your hand in God's
      and begin the long journey home
on the other side of denial.

The Story Behind _The Other Side of Denial_ – _The Other Side of Denial_ is a tribute to the profound impact that my counselor and friend, Dr. Tom Hawkins, had on my healing. A gracious, insightful alumnus of Dallas Theological Seminary, Tom was a gifted teacher and former pastor who I originally met as a guest speaker at our church—before I recognized that I "had issues" or needed healing.

Tom's years of investment in my healing and his influential impact on my identity inspired _The Other Side of Denial_—a poem written on the last full day of his ministry with me, after I had boarded a plane and began this tribute to our work together.

Tom used to say that when a person is in denial about something, they don't know it. But when a person suddenly realizes that they have been in denial—when they understand how they have been deceived or misled about a certain truth or reality—then they are no longer in denial. _That_ is the beginning of the other side of denial.

The Story Behind _Complete_ – The black-and-white drawing of the girl opposite the poem, _The Other Side of Denial_, was produced during a marathon drawing session, long before the poem was written, and years before I was healed. I

chose this drawing to illustrate three of the lines from the end of the poem:

> _And you know you are complete,_
> _and you wrap yourself in joy,_
> _and you cry._

Before my mind was restored to being whole, I rarely cried. As a child I had learned to shut off my tears, because it simply wasn't safe to show my emotions at home. When my broken mind was healed, my emotions were no longer locked down, and I didn't feel compelled to stop my tears—especially tears of joy.

The Story Behind _The Long Journey Home_ – The torn paper/watercolor collage on the opposite page was created after I returned home from my last counseling session with Tom. Suddenly I felt less restraint and took more risks in my art. I no longer approached my work with an expectation of a perfect outcome. For _The Long Journey Home_, I knew that I wanted to convey the sense of freedom I had gained as a result of my healing. This painting symbolizes life's opposing forces of darkness and light, chaos and peace, sorrow and joy. The liberated, resolute little bird is taking flight, in spite of the turbulence surrounding it, towards the light of God's healing power.

"The Long Journey Home"

*...How wide and long
and high and deep
is the love of Christ.*

Ephesians 3:18

"Hiding Place"

You are my hiding place;
You will protect me from trouble
and surround me with
songs of deliverance.

Psalm 32:7

Afterword

While completing the final draft of this book, I was unexpectedly hospitalized with Covid pneumonia for two-and-a-half weeks. For days I could barely breathe, let alone talk without going into violent spells of coughing. When I was finally able to speak again, I had extended conversations with several members of the hospital staff—nurses, occupational therapists, and physical therapists—who took the time to ask what I did for a living. "I'm a retired teacher," I said. "What do you do *now*?" they continued. "I'm a writer and an artist. I was preparing to publish a book when I got sick." In every case, the staff member asked, "What is your book about?" Without hesitation, I responded, "It's about how deep wounds from your past can tear a family apart, and how God can heal those wounds and reunite a family—even after 20 years." "Wow," was always the response, followed by the healthcare worker taking a seat and disclosing aspects of their own family's personal struggles.

My point in mentioning this is to acknowledge that psychological pain—mental and emotional distress—is universal, and people who are generally transparent save their deepest burdens to share with other transparent people who have walked similar paths. Even when an emotionally open person spends years unconsciously pushing away hurtful memories, eventually their longing for authenticity and their aversion to façades will override their habit of remaining unknown to themselves. If you, the reader, recognize that something is "off" in your own life—if you notice that you are floundering in one or more persistently challenging relationships, finding it difficult to trust others, or even doubting your own sanity—you've already begun the journey towards inner healing. Your need for understanding and resolution will drive you to contemplate experiences and relationships that may have damaged your sense of identity and purpose in life. Seeking the truth *now*, despite your deepest fears of what might be uncovered, will give you unprecedented strength and clarity for the future.

The universality of pain and the quest for authentic, purposeful living are two of the main reasons I pursued publishing *A Quarter Past Normal*. This is not a fix-it book or a how-to manual, but a straightforward call to honesty, courage, and action in restoring vitality and wholeness to your body, soul, and spirit.

Although *A Quarter Past Normal* is based upon my own journey of restoration, it is also representative of numerous abuse survivors I've met throughout the years—those who have bravely chosen to tackle the complicated path of inner healing and who deserve recognition as warriors, heroes, and overcomers. On their behalf, there are three final topics that bear special emphasis in this book.

First, when an overcomer commits to long-term counseling, it isn't unusual for that person to be unofficially deemed the *identified* or *designated patient* by their family of origin. Exposing the family secrets—even privately—inevitably generates emotional shockwaves and stirs up shame amongst defensive parents and siblings. When this happens, family members may fall into the double trap of minimizing the entire family's extreme dysfunctions and denying their own unresolved issues. In such family systems, the spotlight of judgment is typically focused upon one person—generally the "scapegoat" or "black sheep of the family"—the one who has most often been blamed for blemishing the family's honor and whose ultimate crime is breaking the family's code of silence.

For overcomers intent on exchanging a destructive past for a life-giving future, I encourage you to privately renounce before God your family's callous judgment, dishonor, and false characterization of *you* as "*The* Problem." Work diligently on your issues—with or without the positive support of your family. But don't accept the lie that *you* are the only family member with problems—or the one with the *worst* problems. Pay attention to your fine-tuned instincts and feelings. Honor and protect your spirit and soul, and whenever you feel minimized, walk away from these demeaning situations with your dignity and bravery still intact. God celebrates the blessing of your existence and is passionately devoted to your wellbeing and the fulfillment of your calling in life. To this end, He has charged His angels with vigilantly advocating on your behalf (Psalm 91:11-12).

A second relevant issue that abuse survivors need to anticipate is the damaging impact that buried trauma—disclosed or undisclosed—will inevitably have upon their children and their marriage. I am profoundly aware of the pain that I caused to my own children due to my deeply buried woundedness. And although we made great memories and enjoyed being in one another's company as a young family, I'm certain that my children were sporadically surprised and distressed by my erratic, "Good Mom-Bad Mom" behavior. Whenever I, as their primary caregiver, was at my emotional tipping point and didn't have the internal reserves to tolerate chaos, fighting, or meanness, my pent-up anger ultimately exploded. Unfortunately, my firstborn child—my daughter—bore the primary brunt of my growing frustrations, which is one reason I decided to seek professional help to unearth the source of my rage. As adults, my children and I have had several one-on-one candid conversations regarding the impact that my destructive childhood had upon their lives. Predictably, *their* mother wounds and father wounds (everyone has them) are now beginning to surface. Despite their miraculous love for me and their forgiveness of my many failings, my grown children—who are raising children of their own—are now compelled to consider the inevitable damage to *their* intimate relationships should they stay in denial about their unresolved woundedness and pretend that everything is forgiven and forgotten, when it hasn't even been talked about.

Regarding the impact of hidden trauma on a marriage, as wounded people, abuse survivors tend to gravitate towards other wounded people, probably because it feels familiar, or maybe because both parties are overly optimistic or just plain blind. As a result of the degrading relationships and experiences from my childhood, I entered marriage, unknowingly allowing my husband to treat me like damaged goods. Every time I felt shamed by him, I resisted confronting him—a lawyer by profession—because I dreaded the debate that would follow.

And yet, as I began to open up to my therapists, my damaged spirit—beaten down after years of being controlled and disrespected in my marriage— suddenly revolted. With my sense of dignity revived, I began affirming my intrinsic value as a human being whenever my husband criticized my weight or my intelligence or my housekeeping skills or my competence as the mother of our children. But instead of acknowledging that his cruel words and behavior *were*, in fact, crushing our relationship and sabotaging our children, my husband persisted in treating me like a sidelined psych patient who wouldn't recognize reality if it hit her in the face. In the complex, uncertain journey of inner healing, when one person changes, everyone around them changes. Reclaiming the identity that God created for you can come at a great price. Yet the alternative is living life in a prison of pain and fear, and that is unacceptable to warriors.

This brings me to my third and final topic—critical to all wounded people: the issue of dignity. Dignity is an attribute that God infuses into our original state of being. It is innate. A sense of dignity tells us that we have value and are worthy of respect—not because of anything we've done to earn it, but simply because God created us. Embracing our dignity allows us to experience honor in our spirit and soul, to recognize our inherent legitimacy as God's handiwork, and to accept the way we're made—regardless of our perceived flaws or known failings. Even if we debase our own dignity through reckless choices, dishonorable behavior, or chronic self-rejection, it doesn't change the value of who we are in God's eyes.

The full impact of dignity and honor didn't fully register with me until I began long-term therapy. As a result of a demoralizing childhood and a marriage that stripped my sense of dignity down to the bare bones, all I could concentrate on before starting therapy was survival. My habit of instinctively blocking out painful thoughts and feelings had helped me to function reasonably well until then, but it had also kept me from recognizing the depth of dishonor I had been tolerating from the people who knew me intimately. In contrast to those primary relationships, the respect extended to me by the mental health professionals who shared in my journey was mind-boggling. For the first time in my life, the people who knew me best—my counselors—didn't treat me like a misfit or an outcast, even after learning about the extent of my fractured, violent past. The awareness of honor I experienced from simply being treated with dignity and not being judged was liberating. I began to see myself as God saw me. And I began to heal.

My parting gift—on the next page—is a blessing that my counselor Tom sent to me after we completed our work together. His life-giving words nullified the damaging impact that my parents' rejection and dishonor once had upon my life. As a fellow advocate for setting captives free, I pass on Tom's blessing to you.

"He will call upon Me, and I will answer him;
I will be with him in trouble,
I will deliver him and honor him."

Psalm 91:15

A Father's Blessing

Dear Beloved Child,

May God bless you with tenderness to hear His voice.

May He bless you with calmness instead of fear.

May He bless you with calm assurance that His power is greater by far than all the power of darkness combined.

May He bless you with the knowledge that He is a good Father who loves to bless His children.

May He bless you with certainty that He has the power to move aside all celestial level evil beings and all those under them who intend to cause you to doubt, become intimidated, and fall into the abyss of fear, terror, and torment.

May the agenda of darkness against you be frustrated, and may He bless you with the fulfillment of His purposes in your life.

May He bless you with provision for your physical needs in accordance with His promise in Matthew 6:33-34, which says, "Seek first His kingdom and His righteousness, and all these things will be given to you as well. Therefore, do not worry about tomorrow, for tomorrow will worry about itself."

May He bless you with His presence and give direction to your path that the year ahead will make you a blessing to many because of His blessings in your life.

May He bless you with an outpouring of His gifts and move you toward healing and intimacy with Himself and a growing closeness, especially, to those of His children whose hearts are tender toward Him.

And may God bless you with favor before Himself and men and lift the curses that previous generations have passed down to you.

From a father in the faith,
Tom

Made in the USA
Coppell, TX
12 December 2021